# NEW

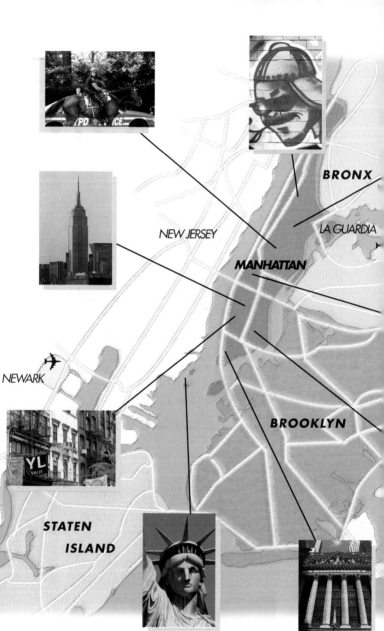

NEW JERSEY

BRONX

LA GUARDIA

MANHATTAN

NEWARK

BROOKLYN

STATEN ISLAND

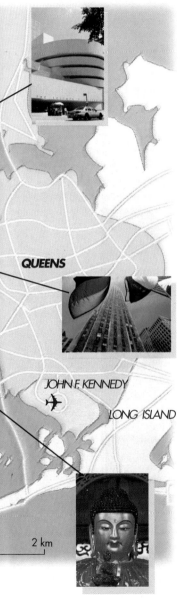

*The image of glass and metal skyscrapers huddled together as the sun sets over Manhattan is one that remains forever etched on the memory.*

**M**anhattan and its tall posse of glass and steel skyscrapers rise high above New York Harbor as symbols of the 'American Dream'.

*NY – an unmistakable skyline.*

# The Big Apple

HARLEM

● Columbia University

HUDSON RIVER

Metropolitan Museum ●
CENTRAL PARK

Times Square ●   ● Rockfeller Center

Empire State Building ●

Washington Square ●   ● United Nations

EAST RIVER

Little Italy

Chinatown

WALL STREET

Brooklyn Bridge

Ellis Island
Twin Towers ●

Liberty Island
● Liberty Statue

*It was in 1524 that Giovanni Verrazano discovered the majestic Bay of New York.*

*Deep navigation channels played an important role in the economic growth of New York and by the beginning of the 19th century it was the country's leading port.*

*The very first inhabitants of 'Maan-a-hat-ta' Island (the land of hills) were members of the Algonquin tribe.*

The wonders of New York's architecture leave many a first-time visitor with a stiff neck. Back in 1524, as he stepped out onto this small island, the Florentine merchant Giovanni Verrazano could hardly have imagined that one day it would come to be the epitome of urban modernity. This new land was named 'Terre d'Angoulême' (Land of Angoulême) in honour of Francis I, of France, in whose name Verrazano had set sail.

*The stars and stripes of the American flag today fly outside many of New York's buildings. Each star represents one of the fifty US states.*

*Trunks and luggage belonging to the first visitors to America.*

*Almost 17 million immigrants from all over the world have passed through Ellis Island. Today, it is an immigration museum enabling the visitor to gain an understanding of the diversity of the American people.*

In 1624, with the creation of a Dutch syndicate trading almost exclusively in furs, the island became known as 'New Amsterdam'. In 1664, however, it was captured by the Duke of York and his troops who immediately renamed it New York. This name was retained even when the city reverted to American rule following the War of American Independence in 1783. It was here that the American Dream was born, attracting several generations of immigrants who came to swell the population of this the most cosmopolitan city in the world. The

*All new immigrants had to enter the country via Ellis Island.*

first port of call for all new arrivals was originally **Castle Clinton**. Seven million people passed through the doors of this former theatre before **Ellis Island** took over as the main reception centre in 1890. Almost half the people living in America have, at some time or other, visited this island which today is home to the immigration museum. It is a highly recommended stopoff for those taking the ferry to Liberty Island.

*In the Museum of the City of New York, on Fifth Avenue, you can visit the remains of a Dutch ship burnt in 1613.*

*Left: The main hall on Ellis Island was where immigrants were kept waiting for hours while all their papers were filled out. The centre itself closed in 1954.*

*The Statue of Liberty holds the Declaration of Independence in its left hand and brandishes a torch in its right as a symbol of liberty enlightening the world.*

*Like a sentry keeping watch, The Lady guards the entrance to New York Harbor.*

From a height of 300 feet (93 metres), the **Statue of Liberty**, nicknamed *The Lady* by New Yorkers, watches over the harbour. A gift from France in 1886, the monument weighs 80 tonnes and is the work of the French artist Bartholdi. Inside its metal framework, designed by the French engineer Eiffel, lie some 354 steps.

*The French artist Bartholdi (1834–1904) dedicated over twenty years of his life to carving the impressive Statue of Liberty.*

*The seven points projecting from the crown of the Statue of Liberty symbolize the seven seas and continents.*

From inside the crown, visitors can enjoy stunning views over the harbour and Ellis Island.

*At the tip of Manhattan, the emblematic figure of George Washington is omnipresent.*

*Some excellent fish dishes are to be found on the menu at Sloppy Louie's, a famous old restaurant at South Street Seaport, made with produce from the nearby market.*

*The maze of streets at the southern tip of Manhattan gives the district a distinctly European feel.*

On the west side of Manhattan, **Battery Park City** stretches along the banks of the Hudson River. This now fashionable area of New York is without skyscrapers or huge imposing structures, populated by much smaller buildings with stone and coloured brick façades. Back in the 19th century, a great deal of activity centred around the quays of **South Street Seaport** on the east bank. Even today, you will

*Ships still come to South Street Seaport to drop anchor in the Bay of New York.*

still come across a number of huge vessels that come to drop anchor in the Bay. South Street Seaport itself has remained a lively district thanks to its many shops and restaurants. Behind the port, the beautiful streets of the Civic Center are full of some surprising contrasts. Not far from St Paul's Chapel, a fine example of Georgian architecture from the 17th century, stands the **Woolworth Building**, which at 790 feet (241 metres) was, until 1930, the tallest building in the world. Erected in 1913, this tower is rather strangely adorned with its gargoyles in the shape of bats.

*The Algonquin Indians were soon driven out of Manhattan. In 1926, Peter Minuit, the first Dutch governor of the colony, took control of their lands in exchange for cloth and trinkets – a 'good deal' in the true spirit of the American Dream.*

*The Brooklyn Bridge is 1600 feet (486 metres) long and contains two double sets of neo-Gothic arches, each measuring 275 feet (84 metres) in height.*

*At first light, it is still worth making time to visit the auctions at the Fulton Fish Market, even if, nowadays, the haul is brought in by refrigerated lorries rather than the boats of old.*

*For twenty years, the magnificent Brooklyn Bridge was the only way of getting from Long Island to Manhattan. Nowadays, there are a dozen or so bridges, such as*

*City Hall, New York's town hall.*

*the Manhattan Bridge, shown here, and many tunnels. Measuring over 4250 feet (1298 metres), the Verrazano Bridge is the longest.*

The Civic Center is also the political heart of New York and home to **City Hall**, the city's town hall. This magnificent building has been the seat of the city council since 1912 and is used by the mayor for receiving important guests. The New York police department and law courts are also found in this district which serves as a popular backdrop for television series.

*A criss-cross of cables and stays on the Brooklyn Bridge.*

Of the dozen or so bridges that cross the East River, the **Brooklyn Bridge** is without a doubt the most famous. When it was opened in 1883, it was the largest suspension bridge in the world and the first to be made of steel. The neo-Gothic arches spanning the East River were destined to link the independent areas of Manhattan and Brooklyn for ever.

*John Roebling, the engineer and designer of the Brooklyn Bridge, was crushed to death by a ferry before work on the bridge began. He was replaced by his son who was paralysed for life with the bends in a decompression accident. Roebling's wife then took over the running of the project which took over 16 years to complete and cost some 20 workers their lives.*

*The neoclassical façade of the present New York Stock Exchange has graced Wall Street since 1903.*

I n the heart of the financial district, the labyrinth of skyscrapers is a rich playground for many of the city's high-flyers and businessmen.

*Lunch break at Federal Hall.*

# *Wall Street*

Greenwich Street

West Street

Broadway

● City Hall

Park Row

Brooklyn Bridge

World Financial Center ●

Barclay Street

● Woolworth Building

● World Trade Center

Twin Towers ●

● AT&T Building

Water Street

Trinity Church ✝

● Federal Reserve Bank

Federal Hall ●

● Chase Manhattan Bank

Wall Street

HUDSON RIVER

EAST RIVER

● Castle Clinton

BATTERY PARK

*This wonderful dome with marble columns stands in the centre of Federal Hall.*

In contrast with the rest of Manhattan, the streets at the southern end of the island do not follow a regular grid system, reflecting instead the layout established by the first settlers who, on their arrival, erected houses in a somewhat haphazard way.

*Wall Street at rush hour. This is the domain of the city's stockbrokers who can often be seen rushing around frantically at all hours of the day.*

From a very early date, Wall Street became an important centre for business and politics. In 1789, George Washington, the first president of the United States, made his investiture

*A statue of Washington stands on the steps of Federal Hall, on the very spot from where he made his inauguration speech when he was elected to become the first president of the United States in 1789.*

speech on the spot where **Federal Hall** now stands. This classical building, which once housed the American customs authorities, today contains a museum dedicated to the Constitution. The **New York Stock Exchange** is located at 68 Wall Street in a veritable neoclassical temple completely devoted to finance. Since its creation in 1903, Wall Street has remained the world's leading centre for international trade where several million securities change hands each day. Over the years, its crashes and booms have made and broken some of the world's largest fortunes.

## The New York Stock Exchange

Industrialists and shopkeepers began exchanging securities as far back as 1790 in the area around Wall Street. These transactions, however, were carried out without any official rules or regulations. In 1792, a group of 24 brokers decided to restrict the exchange of securities, trading only between themselves. This association marked the official start of the New York Stock Exchange. Today the quotations are computerized and stored on the central SuperDOT computer. The Stock Exchange consists of 17 syndicates, made up of 22 sections of brokers and terminals that determine the quotations of ten companies. Every day, 200 million securities are exchanged on behalf of 2000 companies.

*Today, a place at the New York Stock Exchange can cost anything up to one million dollars. For those wishing just to visit, the entrance is on Broad Street.*

*Trinity Church was built in 1846.*

*This sea goddess decorates the entrance to the AT&T Building which used to house the offices of the American Telephone and Telegraph company.*

*On Wall Street, the bull represents a rise in prices and the bear a fall. Needless to say, the only bronze statue in the district is that of a bull.*

The gold reserves of many countries are guarded under tight security in the basement of the **Federal Reserve Bank**. It is in this 'bank of banks', modelled on the architecture of a Florentine palace, that most American coins are minted. Away from the hustle and bustle, in the cemetery of **Trinity Church**, lie a number of famous people.

*Each day on Wall Street, limousines pass each other with a disdainful air. This area has always been at the very heart of the business and political activities of the city. Wall Street itself takes its name from the palings erected in 1653 by the governor Peter Stuyvesant to keep out British assailants.*

21

*'The Big Apple', the nickname of New York, was coined by the jazz musicians of the 1930s. The expression became popular in the 1970s when it was used in an advertising campaign.*

*On Printing House Square, the statue of Benjamin Franklin holding a copy of the Pennsylvania Gazette reminds us that the man who helped to draw up the Declaration of Independence was also the father of the American press.*

*By far the largest strongroom in the world, the size of a football pitch, is found in the tower of the Chase Manhattan Bank. Security systems have transformed this building into something resembling an impenetrable fortress.*

*At the foot of the Equitable Building.*

The office blocks in this area are often overshadowed by the **Equitable Building**. In 1915, legal proceedings were instituted against its developers by companies who had been deprived of natural light. Ever since, a law has governed the maximum height of sky-scrapers. Not that this stood in the way of the Twin Towers being built!

*Skyscrapers reach higher and higher into the skies. In the foreground, the* Group of four trees, *a statue by Jean Dubuffet, stands at the foot of the Chase Manhattan Bank.*

*A lift takes visitors to the panoramic restaurant at the top of Tower 1 in 58 seconds. Just long enough to work up an appetite!*

*The twin towers dominate the World Trade Center which is home to 450 companies.*

At over 1300 feet (409 metres), the **Twin Towers** of the World Trade Center were for many years the tallest buildings in the world. The 110 floors are home to 50,000 employees, who, when not working, can enjoy the benefits of a winter garden, restaurants and boutiques. A lift will take you to the restaurant (Tower 1) or the panoramic viewing gallery (Tower 2) situated on the top floor in less than a minute!

*On August 7, 1974, Philippe Petit walked from one tower to the other on a tight-rope, some 1300 feet (409 metres) up in the air.*

*Musicians and artists are often found performing in the streets of this the capital of entertainment.*

*The banks of the Hudson River at the marina in front of the World Financial Center.*

*For those looking for a quick bite to eat, hot dogs and bagels can be bought on almost any street corner. Local businessmen, however, are much more likely to go to the McDonald's at 160 Broadway. In what has to be one of the most luxurious fast-food restaurant in the world, you can order a Big Mac whilst keeping your eye on the share prices which are flashed up on a screen.*

The banks of the Hudson, once shunned by tourists, have been given a new lease of life since the building of the **World Financial Center**, a veritable masterpiece of civil architecture. Under an enormous glass and steel ceiling, the visitor will discover a winter garden, shops and restaurants. Free shows, concerts and ballets are

*The spectacular winter garden.*

*The large mouth of the Hudson River is an ecological oasis favoured by sturgeon and bass that come to spawn upstream and are then caught not far from the Statue of Liberty. In summer, warmed by the Gulf Stream, the area attracts tropical fish such as grouper and butterfly fish – a veritable godsend for the peregrine falcons that live among the glass and steel façades of the buildings.*

organized in the atrium designed by Cesar Pelli & Associates. In spite of this, there is a serious air about the place since the World Financial Center is also home to a number of offices linked to the World Trade Center. All of which goes to prove that in the USA, more than any other country in the world, people like to mix business with pleasure.

*Large three-storey Victorian houses rub shoulders with huge skyscrapers, reminding the visitor that the skyline at the southern end of Manhattan is forever changing. Indeed, the city is actually spreading into the sea: Battery Park, South Street Seaport and the World Financial Center are all built on reclaimed land.*

*Palm trees from the Mohave Desert stand proud in the World Financial Center.*

*The climate in New York can be quite harsh and varied. Temperatures can range from −25°C (−13°F) in winter to +41°C (106°F) in summer.*

*The imposing Twin Towers of the World Trade Center took ten years to build.*

Next to the World Trade Center stands **St Paul's Chapel**, the only church left on Manhattan that was built before Independence (1776). The main body of the church, the oldest religious building in New York, dates from 1764, whilst the tower and portico were added in 1794. After more than two centuries, the pew where the father of American Independence, George Washington, came to sit and pray is still there.

*The Twin Towers stand head and shoulders above the other buildings in New York. Here they look down on their older cousin, the Brooklyn Bridge.*

*In the heart of Greenwich Village, town houses complete with pediments, columned porches and walled gardens recall a glorious past.*

F rom Chinatown to Chelsea, the 'villages' of New York mix the quaint with the modern to produce some highly surprising contrasts.

*Having fun in Washington Square.*

# Village Life

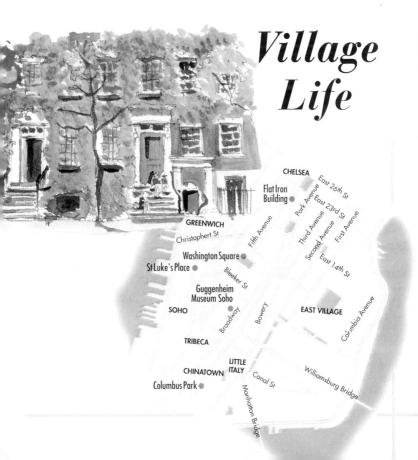

CHELSEA

East 26th St

East 23rd St

Flat Iron Building

Park Avenue

Third Avenue

Second Avenue

First Avenue

GREENWICH

Christophert St

Fifth Avenue

East 14th St

Washington Square

St Luke's Place

Bleeker St

Guggenheim Museum Soho

SOHO

Broadway

Bowery

EAST VILLAGE

Columbia Avenue

TRIBECA

LITTLE ITALY

CHINATOWN

Canal St

Williamsburg Bridge

Columbus Park

Manhattan Bridge

*Murals depict the way of life of Chinatown's residents.*

*The Peking Duck House, at 22 Mott Street, is a treat for lovers of Chinese cuisine, serving the best Peking duck and dim sum in America. At the end of the meal, fortune cookies containing short proverbs on small pieces of paper will leave you with something to think about.*

In the heart of the Lower East Side, the buildings of **Chinatown** look like those of Macao or Beijing, recreating the setting of a typical Asian community. With its banks and telephone boxes in the shape of pagodas, this colourful area offers visitors a taste of the Far East without leaving New York. Many of its 80,000 Sino-American inhabitants still appear to be living according to their age-old customs and traditions.

*The Eastern States Buddhist Temple at 64b Mott Street contains over one hundred golden effigies of Buddha. The faithful come here to bring offerings and light candles.*

*As in Thailand, shops offer a wide range of designer watches, jewellery and leather goods at low prices...but beware of imitations.*

*The market stalls are full of ducks, prawn crackers and fresh vegetables.*

With the street names, shop signs and menus all in Chinese, it is often difficult to find your way around the Asian district, but this just adds further to the charm and mystery of Chinatown. At the start of the 20th century, the area was terrorized by secret organizations such as the Tongs and the Mafia. Doyers Street even became known as **Bloody Angle** because of the number of fights between rival gangs that took place there.

*At the first full moon following January 21, the Chinese celebrate New Year and a carnival atmosphere comes to Chinatown: long paper dragons dance to the rhythm of drums, fireworks light up the night sky and acrobats vie with each other in skill.*

*An abundance of fresh vegetables, colours and smells at Dean and Deluca's.*

*Enjoy some of the city's finest cappuccinos, home-made ice cream, bread and cakes at Ferrara's, 195–201 Grand Street (open since 1892) and at Luna's, 112 Mulberry Street. Be warned: the portions are not for those with a small appetite!*

Surrounded by Chinatown, the area known as **Little Italy** now covers no more than a few streets. New York's Italian population, which totalled 150,000 before World War II, has today been reduced to around 5000. In September, on Mulberry Street, various events and processions take place over a period of eleven days and nights to celebrate the festival of San Gennaro, the patron saint of Naples.

*Since 1919, the colours of the Italian flag have adorned the façade of Puglia's. In this area, many restaurants and grocer's have retained their Latin charm.*

*The 'brownstones' lining St Luke's Place and Christopher Street owe their name to the original colour of their walls.*

*In the villages, the buildings retain slightly more human dimensions.*

In **Greenwich Village**, the quiet winding streets lined with trees and lamp-posts have a European, almost provincial, air about them, escaping as they do the grid layout favoured by modern American town planners. In 'The Village', as it is known by New Yorkers, there are still signs of the old plots of land and streams that once divided up this district. Today, the district of SoHo is a veritable Mecca for alternative artists.

*Back in the 19th century, Edgar Allan Poe and Mark Twain were seduced by the many charms of Greenwich Village. In the 1960s, it became a popular haunt of artists, writers like Tennessee Williams and singers such as Bob Dylan and Joan Baez.*

*New York's villages are a treasure trove of culture. At the end of Greenwich Ave, Jefferson Courthouse Market Library is a must for bibliophiles.*

*In SoHo, grocers', florists' and artists' stalls bring colour to the streets.*

*A modern work of art in SoHo.*

*Creating a look for yourself in New York is an absolute must and shops selling new and second-hand clothes are found on every street corner. In SoHo,*

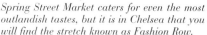

*Spring Street Market caters for even the most outlandish tastes, but it is in Chelsea that you will find the stretch known as Fashion Row.*

At first glance, there is nothing to suggest that the delicatessens and fashionable cafés of **SoHo** (short for South of Houston) have been built in 19th-century warehouses. Back in the 1970s, these former industrial enclaves were all threatened with demolition, but today they attract the fashionable set who themselves have taken over from bohemian artists.

*The walls of SoHo also double up as canvases for street artists.*

Forced out by rising rents, the latter moved to **TriBeCa** (short for Triangle Below Canal Street). After the exodus of industry in the 1970s, the cast-iron buildings attracted artists looking for space and light. Today, the spirit of Andy Warhol lives on in these studios that have now been converted into apartments and art galleries.

*Cast-iron buildings with their carved steel façades and light roomy studios are what have made SoHo famous.*

*Paradoxically, however, these buildings originally sought to imitate brick in their use of paint mixed with sand. Such has been their success that a number of brick buildings now strive to imitate cast iron!*

On Sundays, Canal Street, Essex, Delancey and Orchard Markets all have tempting offers on clothes, jewellery and electrical goods.

At the junction of SoHo, Greenwich and Chelsea, Bleeker Street is famous for its jazz clubs, record shops and many specialist bookshops.

Back in the 19th century, the Astor, Stuyvesant and Vanderbilt families brought a certain respectability to the East Village before the upper classes decided to move north in 1900. During the swinging sixties, hippies moved into the area and transformed St Mark's Place into the Mecca of fashion and counterculture.

Fashionable Tex-Mex in Chelsea.

Ever since the 1960s, the **East Village** has been the respective home of the beat generation, hippies and punk rockers. Above all, however, the district has retained many traces of its original inhabitants, the Germans, Jews and Puerto Ricans. At the corner of Broadway and 5th Avenue stands the impressive sight of the **Flatiron Building**.

*Ever since 1902, when its 300 feet (91 metres) made it the tallest building in the world, the Flatiron Building has stood at the corner of Broadway and 5th Avenue.*

*In New York, the traffic is relatively well organized. Roads are largely reserved for public transport and yellow taxis.*

I nternationally prestigious and animated at any hour of the day or night, Midtown is the veritable nerve centre of New York.

*A fleet of taxis on Broadway.*

# *Midtown*

# *and 5th Ave*

*The image of planes attacking King Kong on the Empire State Building is now part of cinema legend. A bomber did actually crash into the tower, however, in 1945.*

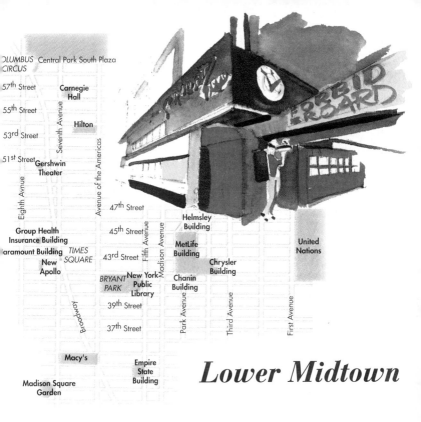

COLUMBUS CIRCLE
Central Park South Plaza
57th Street
Carnegie Hall
55th Street
Seventh Avenue
Hilton
53rd Street
51st Street
Gershwin Theater
Avenue of the Americas
Eighth Avnue
47th Street
Helmsley Building
Group Health Insurance Building
45th Street
Fifth Avenue
Madison Avenue
MetLife Building
aramount Building
TIMES SQUARE
43rd Street
Chrysler Building
United Nations
New Apollo
BRYANT PARK
New York Public Library
Chanin Building
Park Avenue
Third Avenue
First Avenue
Broadway
39th Street
37th Street
Macy's
Empire State Building
Madison Square Garden

# *Lower Midtown*

The sky was, quite literally, the limit for those responsible for designing the various buildings of Midtown. The mythical spire of the Empire State Building rises proudly

*Building work on the Empire State Building, designed as a solution to the problem of over-population, began just weeks before the Wall Street Crash of 1929. Thanks to the number of visitors it attracted, the developers man aged to escape bankruptcy.*

above an area that covers more space vertically than it does horizontally.

*The many different departments of Macy's, the largest department store in the world, stretch over a whole block, not far from the Garment Center.*

*The red star used as the shop's logo was inspired by the tattoo of its founder, Rowland Macy, a former whaler who opened the first shop in 1857.*

*The Empire State Building.*

With its 1450 feet (443 metres) of granite and stylized aluminium, the **Empire State Building** was, for many years, the tallest building in the world. The spire that tops the 102 floors, has, over the years, been used as a mooring post for airships, then as a radio aerial. The viewing platform at the top is visited each year by some two million people.

*From the top of the Empire State Building, you can see for over 80 miles (125 km) on a clear day. By far the best time to admire the view, however, is as the sun is setting and the surrounding buildings, such as the New York Life Insurance building, shown here, are lighting up.*

*Not far from the Empire State Building stands the Metropolitan Life Insurance Building with its four enormous clock faces.*

*The New York Public Library; a temple of knowledge and learning.*

On 5th Avenue, the **New York Public Library** is a veritable jewel of beaux arts style. This library originally housed the collections of James Lenox, the speculator, and J. J. Astor and today has around 90 miles (140 kilometres) of shelf space for storing two million books and 10,000 periodicals. The treasures of the collection include a draft of the Declaration of Independence signed by Thomas Jefferson, a

*The New York Public Library, was designed by the architects Carrère & Hastings and cost $9 million to build.*

*To celebrate the World Exhibition of 1853, a copy of London's Crystal Palace was built where Bryant Park now stands. The park itself was laid out after the glasshouse was destroyed by fire. It is the only area of greenery in this part of Manhattan.*

The entrance to the New York Public Library is carefully guarded by Prudence and Fortitude, two lions in pink marble carved by the sculptor Edward Clark Potter and named by Mayor LaGuardia. The way to knowledge certainly deserves a triumphal entrance and the main façade, with its triple arcade topped with a carved group, appropriately recalls a triumphal arch with columns. The fresco that decorates this entrance was carved by Weyland Barrlet and represents an allegory of knowledge. Depicted from left to right are History, Theatre, Poetry, Religion, Literature and Philosophy. As for the fountains surrounding the building, they are the work of Frederick McMonnies.

Gutenberg Bible, a Shakespeare first edition and a handwritten letter from Christopher Columbus. The reading room on the third floor can hold up to 500 people and still has its original Tiffany lamps. The entrance is guarded by Prudence and Fortitude, two lions carved by Potter. Behind the New York Public Library, an extension has been built under Bryant Park. These extra miles of shelf space enable over three million works to be stored. In the 1960s, **Bryant Park** was a meeting place for drug addicts and dealers. In 1989, it was cleaned up and transformed into a place of relaxation.

*The gleaming Chrysler Building symbolizes the glittering rise of Walter Chrysler, the king of the automobile.*

*Sailors enjoying leave on Broadway.*

# 42nd Street to Broadway

Across the width of Manhattan, 42nd Street reveals the many different faces of New York. From the Chrysler Building to Times Square, luxury and decadence

alternate with a speed to match the breathtaking pace of life in the city.

*In New York, time is of the essence. At Bloomingdale's, the window displays are changed almost every week. An appointment with a lawyer lasts between five and ten minutes and it takes just twelve minutes to down a Coke and a burger! There is no let up in the Big Apple where you are forced to live for the moment.*

*Sculptures in the park of the United Nations symbolize peace and non-violence.*

*For three months every year, all the member states of the UN attend a meeting of the General Assembly in an enormous room containing 2070 seats, all with headsets. Members of the Security Council, meanwhile, meet around a table in the shape of*

*a horseshoe. Nations are generally seated in alphabetical order, but the places on the front rows are drawn from a hat.*

To the east of Lower Midtown, the monolithic outline of the **UN Headquarters** stands on the banks of the East River. When it was built in 1945, only 52 flags flew on the site measuring some 17 acres (7 hectares). Today, some 180 member states benefit from the status of extraterritoriality on the land obtained by the

*The impressive MetLife Building.*

*Built to the glory of the automobile industry, the chrome gargoyles of the Chrysler Building recall the emblem of the 1929 Chrysler Plymouth.*

*The Chrysler Building contains a hall full of display cabinets in nickel-plated steel in which the symbolic eagle keeps watch.*

international organization thanks to the 8.5 million dollars donated by the industrialist, John D. Rockefeller. At the end of **Park Avenue**, it is impossible to miss the colossal MetLife Building. Originally built as the head-quarters of the airline company Pan Am, the dark imposing outline blocks out the sun, casting a shadow over this elegant avenue.

*Each of the 77 floors of the Chrysler Building is decorated with ornate wheels and radiator caps. The art deco spire was added to the 'bodywork' at the last moment and in the strictest secrecy in order to make the building taller than the rival premises of the Bank of America.*

*A detail from one of the many frescoes that decorate the Chanin Building.*

*With a choice from 1800 rooms, a night at the sumptuous Waldorf Astoria is a must for any pretender to the White House.*

*The somewhat flashy façade of the Helmsley Building is largely the work of Leona, the wife of the millionaire Harry Helmsley.*

Among the many structures overshadowed by the tall MetLife Building is the **Helmsley Building.** With its pyramid-shaped roof, it enjoys a central position on the imposing Park Avenue, surrounded by greenery and flowers and spanning the road and its constant flow of traffic. Buses, underground stations, shops and businesses are all banned from this avenue which is one of the most sought-after addresses in New York.

*Mythical figures from Ancient Rome flank the clock on the Helmsley Building.*

The elegant **St Bartholomew's Church**, with its pink bricks, forecourt and polychrome dome, is perfectly in keeping with the sophisticated surroundings. The outer portal, a copy of the one at the provincial abbey of St-Gilles-du-Garde in France, compliments the neo-Byzantine style of the rest of the building which provides the regular setting for jazz, choral and organ concerts. Nearby, the **Waldorf Astoria** has retained much of the glamour of its glittering past, when it was frequented by the likes of the Duke and Duchess of Kent and Winston Churchill.

*New York is a city that never sleeps. At any hour of the day or night you can go shopping, have a meal or see a show. For the more reckless visitor, the underground runs all night too!*

*The hustle and bustle of rush hour at Grand Central Terminal.*

The glass walls of **Lever House** reflect the other buildings of Park Avenue. This listed building was the first glass structure to be built in New York. The material was chosen to symbolize the purity of the Lever brothers' soaps and detergents and the modernity of the design caused quite a sensation when it was opened in 1952. Today, avant-garde buildings, such as the 900-feet-high (270-metre-high) offices of

*Waiting in the hall of Grand Central Terminal, travellers have the chance to flick through the day's papers. New Yorkers are reputed to be enthusiastic newspaper readers.*

*Roman gods are everywhere to be found in New York. Minerva, Hercules and Mercury look down from the pediment of the façade of Grand Central Terminal on 42nd Street.*

## A famous station

In Grand Central Terminal, the scurrying crowd of travellers keep one eye on the four-faced clock that stands above the information desk. The ceiling of the enormous hall depicts the vault of heaven by Paul Helleu. The French artist, drawing inspiration from a manuscript dating from the Middle Ages, reproduced a sky dotted with 2500 stars in which the principal constellations light up. Everything, from the grand marble staircase, inspired by the one in the Opéra in Paris, to the bronze ticket offices, recalls the great age of American rail travel. Lovers of seafood may like to visit the popular Oyster Bar on the main concourse.

Citycorp are a common sight. This incredible building, the fourth highest in New York, is topped with a bevelled roof that was originally designed to harness solar energy. On Park Avenue and 42nd Street, at the instigation of the railway tycoon Cornelius Vanderbilt, a large station, **Grand Central Terminal**, was completed in 1913 as an answer to the problem of increasing rail traffic and the introduction of new electric trains. A fine example of beaux arts style, the building contains 48 underground tracks on which more than 500,000 commuters travel every day.

*In the heart of theatreland, a host of neon signs and adverts light up Times Square. The giant screen was installed for the presidential elections of 1928.*

*In Times Square, adverts try to out do each other in colour and visual effects.*

**Times Square** is above all famous for its theatres and should be visited preferably at night to see the mass of neon lights and flashing signs. At the corner of Broadway and 7th Avenue, a giant screen fronts the building that used to house the offices of the prestigious New York Times. Like most other respectable companies, the city's newspaper has now left the area, chased out by the invasion of porn cinemas and sex shops.

*The enormous screen in Times Square gives passers-by information on such diverse things as the latest news, the level of the country's foreign debt and the number of people who have been shot.*

*Broadway: the district of music halls is a popular backdrop for films.*

*The programme of all shows currently on in New York is published in the New York Times and the Village Voice. For the more successful shows, you may need to book a few months in advance. On Broadway, TKTS kiosks offer cut-price tickets.*

On December 31, New Yorkers gather at the foot of the New York Times Building down which an illuminated ball falls to mark the arrival of the New Year. This area was renovated during the 1980s, much to the delight of theatre lovers. Today there is a wide choice, from successful musicals to avant-garde drama and the classics. There is also much to choose from on one of the many giant cinema screens.

*Musical after musical comes to Broadway. Some stay only a couple of months, others, such as Cats, have been here for almost 20 years.*

*Carnegie Hall is said to have the finest acoustics in the world.*

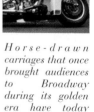

As you walk up 7th Avenue, you will pass in front of **Carnegie Hall**, the world-famous concert hall. When it was opened back in 1891, this neo-Renaissance building was one of the first in New York to be dedicated solely to music. Reputed

*Horse-drawn carriages that once brought audiences to Broadway during its golden era have today been replaced by powerful machines.*

to have the finest acoustics in the world, it remains associated with some of the biggest names, from Tchaikovsky, Caruso and Toscanini to Bill Haley and the Beatles.

*In the cinema that used to be located on the ground floor of the Paramount Building, stars such as Frank Sinatra came to iron out any problems with their shows.*

A stone's throw away from the Mecca of music stands the **Paramount Building**, dedicated to the world of cinema. This Pharaonic structure, resembling an Aztec pyramid, was built in 1927 in pure art deco style. It once contained a huge cinema and a viewing platform, both of which no longer exist. Another throwback to the golden age of Broadway is the New Amsterdam Theater, once home to the legendary Ziegfield Follies. Like many of the theatres along 42nd Street that were hit by economic crisis, it was eventually transformed into a second-rate cinema.

## Carnegie Hall

It was the millionaire Andrew Carnegie who financed the building of the famous concert hall that carries his name. At that time, it was situated on the outskirts of the city but still managed to attract a huge crowd when it opened in 1891. This might have had something to do with the fact that Tchaikovsky was conducting. For many years, Carnegie Hall was home to the New York Philharmonic, under the baton of many famous conductors such as Toscanini, Stokowski, Walter and Bernstein. At the end of the 1950s, developers tried to convert it into office space. A campaign, led by the violinist Isaac Stern, however, mobilized the whole of New York and the plans were dropped.

*The slender outline of the Rockefeller Center represents a new approach to city planning. More than just an office block, it also attracts those out for a stroll.*

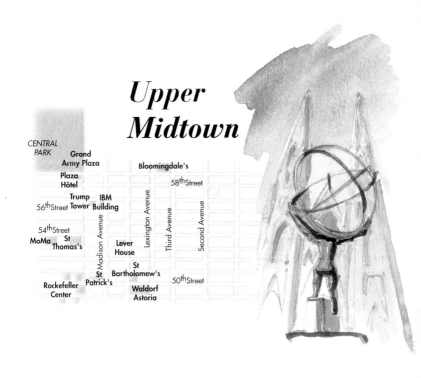

# Upper Midtown

CENTRAL PARK

Grand Army Plaza

Bloomingdale's

Plaza Hôtel

58th Street

Trump Tower

IBM Building

56th Street

Madison Avenue

Lexington Avenue

Third Avenue

Second Avenue

54th Street

MoMa

St Thomas's

Lever House

St Bartholomew's

50th Street

Rockefeller Center

St Patrick's

Waldorf Astoria

In this chic district, the 'City of Glass' becomes a shop window in which, wealth and excess are shamelessly flaunted. In this area, the ultimate symbol of the American Dream is to have a skyscraper named after you!

*The fashionable shopping district of Upper Midtown exudes New York style and luxury. Famous addresses, such as Christie's auction rooms and Saks Fifth Avenue, have been the arbiters of taste and style for many generations.*

## Paste on Diamond Row

The block on 47th Street between 5th Avenue and 6th Avenue has acquired the flash nickname of Diamond Row. Here, all the famous jeweller's display their glittering wares under the watchful eye of uniformed guards. Nevertheless, lovers of gold and jewels can find some dazzling bargains in one of the many small jeweller's, run, for the most part, by immigrants from central Europe.

*This carved plaque, entitled News, is found at the entrance to the Associated Press Building, which, like many other radio and TV stations, is found in the Rockefeller Center. Free invitations to the studio recording of shows are regularly given out to the public on Rockefeller Plaza.*

Trump Tower, the Sony Building, the Rockefeller Center... The district of Upper Midtown is packed with buildings which vie with each other in height to convey the success of their owners. In this forest of skyscrapers, wealth is paraded and shops sparkle like diamonds, whilst the sky is blocked out by an imposing number of heady buildings. Ever since the end of the 19th century, the area has been the privileged home of some of the country's richest families, such as the Astors and the Vanderbilts. During the 1950s, an architectural revolution began in New York.

*In spring, the ice rink at the Rockefeller Plaza is transformed into a colourful terrace.*

*This bronze Atlas carrying a globe is found at the entrance to the International Building and is the figure head of the Rockefeller Center. It is the work of Lee Lawrie.*

Within this district, sky-scrapers suddenly began springing up like mush-rooms, transforming it from a residential neigh-bourhood into an inter-national business centre. 'International' is, in fact, the term used to describe this style of architecture. Horizontal and vertical lines are the order of the day and the preferred materials are glass, steel and concrete. These monoliths are all several hundred feet tall.

*A classical fresco graces the entrance hall to the Rockefeller Center.*

The **Rockefeller Center** represents the largest collection of skyscrapers anywhere in the world. Nineteen buildings and a total of 557 floors and 67 lifts spread over three blocks and house offices, shops, auditoriums, bars and restaurants. Built by

*The Rockefeller Center owes its art deco style and classical frescoes to Nelson Aldrich Rockefeller, the art lover and youngest son of John D. Rockefeller.*

the millionaire John D. Rockefeller in 1930 on the site of a former botanical garden, this cultural and commercial centre became a listed building in 1985. At that time, the

*In the 1930s there was a revival of interest in ancient civilizations, illustrated here in the shape of Wisdom by Lee Lawrie. In the Rockefeller Center, images from classical mythology contrast sharply with communal architecture, once considered to be so radical.*

## A giant complex

The Rockefeller Center is the largest building project that has ever been undertaken. Back in 1929, John Davidson Rockefeller signed a 24-year lease with the former owners of the property, the University of Columbia. Since then, the lease has been renewed until 2069. The initial project almost failed to get off the ground due to the Wall Street Crash of 1929, but whilst neighbouring shops were closing down one after the other, the Rockefeller Center was being transformed into an enormous building site. In order to leave room for wide open spaces outside, car parks, subway stations and shopping arcades were all built underground, as far as 85 feet (26 metres) below the surface.

commission in charge of listing went as far as to describe it as 'the heart of New York'! The final building, west of 6th Avenue, was completed in 1973.

Every year in winter, the art deco surroundings of the Rockefeller Plaza become the setting for an open-air ice rink. At Christmas, under the watchful eye of Atlas, a bronze statue by Lee Lawrie, skaters glide along peacefully beneath fir trees groaning under the weight of garlands. In summer, the rink is transformed into a terrace where New York society come to quench their thirst.

*Modern art posters outside the Museum of Modern Art.*

*The exhibits at the Museum of Modern Art include Picasso's Les Demoiselles d'Avignon, the painting that launched the Cubist movement, surrealist paintings by Dali, sculptures by Brancusi and Rodin and the sensual smile of Andy Warhol's Marylin.*

Museum Mile runs the length of Central Park beginning with the Museum of Modern Art, or **MoMA**, at the corner of 55th Street. When it opened in 1929, this was the only museum dedicated totally to modern art in the world. Financed by wealthy sponsors, it still houses one of the richest collections of exhibits anywhere in the world, ranging from paintings and drawings to film and photography.

*At MoMA, paintings, sculptures, photographs, architecture and design trace the history of a century of aesthetic quests.*

*Once inside St Patrick's Cathedral, it is easy to forget that 5th Avenue and its incessant traffic is just a few feet away.*

*The statue of St Patrick, the patron saint of Ireland.*

Opposite the Rockefeller Center and Radio City Music Hall, amid the huddle of skyscrapers, stands **St Patrick's Cathedral**, dedicated to the patron saint of Ireland. Built in the image of Cologne Cathedral, with its 300-feet (100-metre) spires, this neo-Gothic religious building was, in the middle of last century, intended for use by students from Columbia University.

*Not far from the Lady Chapel, in which stained-glass windows represent the mysteries of the rosary, stands a wonderful pietà by William O. Partridge. Once inside the 9-tonne bronze doors of St Patrick's, the visitor is struck by the intense atmosphere of quiet meditation.*

*Jewellery from all over the world is displayed in the windows of Harry Winston's.*

*Following Cartier, who opened a shop in the home of the millionaire Morton F. Plant in exchange for a superb pearl necklace, many jewellers have moved to this area which was once inhabited by members of high society.*

As you make your way up **5th Avenue** towards Central Park, shop windows display one luxury after another. Sak's Fifth Avenue (between 49th and 50th Street) is famous for its window displays at Christmas and sells beautiful furs, jewellery and clothes. Further along, Brentano's bookshop was formerly Scribner's & Sons, the house that published the works of Scott Fitzgerald and Ernest Hemingway.

*A provocative mixture of luxury and size on 5th Avenue. These shop dummies are strategically positioned to attract your attention.*

*To have a pied-à-terre in this tower costs a small fortune and is only affordable by the fabulously wealthy few, such as Steven Spielberg.*

*Upper Midtown is dotted with large luxury hotels, such as the Waldorf Astoria.*

At the entrance to **Trump Tower**, the epitome of a monument to the glory of capitalism, gold letters spell out the name of the property baron Donald J. Trump. The building, completed in 1983, is a true product of the consumer society. Pink marble, glittering copperplate and artificial waterfalls decorate the atrium and shopping arcade which boasts many luxury boutiques and cafés over six floors.

*Situated next to Trump Tower, Tiffany's, the jeweller's, was the inspiration behind Truman Capote's novel Breakfast at Tiffany's.*

*Standing at the corner of 5th Avenue, horse-drawn carriages wait to take visitors on a tour of Central Park.*

*The extraordinary spiral building of the Guggenheim Museum is dedicated to modern art and design.*

A long the east side of Central Park, 5th Ave is home to museums that contain some of the finest collections in the world.

*Museum Mile starts here.*

# *Museum Mile*

International Center of Photography

Jewish Museum

Cooper-Hewitt Museum

National Academy of Design

Guggenheim Museum

Metropolitan Museum of Art

Fifth Avenue

Madison Avenue

Park Avenue

Lexington Avenue

Third Avenue

East 88th Street

CENTRAL PARK

Whitney Museum of American Art

East 76th Street

Frick Collection

Asia Collection

Second Avenue

East 74th Street

First Avenue

York Avenue

East 62nd Street

East 59th Street

*The imposing neoclassical façade of the Metropolitan Museum of Art.*

*Under a glass pyramid, the Lehman collection, bequeathed to the city in 1971, contains works which date from the period of the Renaissance up to 19th century: drawings, furniture, Venetian glass, enamelware and bronzes.*

On the edge of Central Park, the **'Met'** (Metropolitan Museum of Art) stands large and proud. One of the biggest museums in the United States, it has continued to grow ever since it was built in 1870. At the beginning of the 20th century, a neoclassical façade was added to adorn the main entrance and numerous wings have subsequently been built. The most recent is dedicated to French Impressionists.

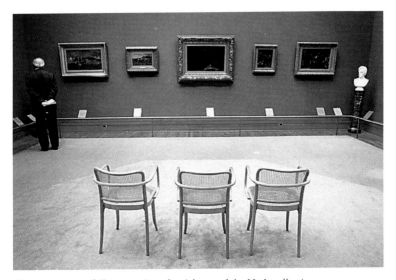

*You need time to fully appreciate the richness of the Met's collections.*

The Met has almost three million works of art in total, most of which have come from wealthy American benefactors. Five thousand years of artistic creation from every continent is exhibited in an area covering 111 acres (45 hectares). The 230 rooms and galleries contain outstanding collections of primitive and Islamic art, art from the Far East, Egyptian, Greek and Roman antiques as well as some surprising weapons and armour dating from the Middle Ages. Forty five thousand patterns from the Fashion Institute retrace the history of clothing over the centuries.

*It was only as recently as 1987 that part of the Met was given over to modern art. Only exceptional works of art are exhibited, such as those by Picasso, Klee and Pollock, as well as the last self-portrait by Andy Warhol. The collection of statues exhibited on the top floor is renewed each year.*

*Millions of visitors pass through the majestic entrance hall of the Metropolitan Museum of Art each year.*

*The arms and armoury room.*

*The Astor courtyard on the first floor of the museum is home to a Ming-style garden, created in 1979 by Chinese craftsmen following traditional techniques. This was the first Sino-American cultural exchange of its kind.*

The gallery dedicated to musical instruments contains some rare Stradivarius violins and unusual instruments from all over the world. The pride of the Met, however, remains its collection of 3000 paintings by major European artists, including Botticelli, Brueghel, Rembrandt, El Greco, Vermeer, La Tour *(La Diseuse de Bonne Aventure)*, Watteau, Goya, Ingres, Manet *(En Bateau)*, Van Gogh *(Cypresses)* and Picasso *(Gertrude Stein)*.

*For those whose thirst for culture has not been quenched by a visit to the Met, there is the choice of the Jewish Museum, specializing in Jewish culture, the International Center of Photography or the Museo del Barrio which organizes various talks and exhibitions on Latin American art.*

*Mobiles by Calder hang from the ceiling of the Guggenheim.*

The **Guggenheim Museum** is dedicated to modern art but unlike MoMA, the surprising spiral shape of this 'temple to the spirit' is in itself the first exhibit. Housing works of art from the 19th and 20th centuries, the visit begins at the top of the rotunda and follows the spiral ramp down to the ground floor. For many visitors, the building proves to be as breathtaking as many of the collections it contains.

*The giant rotunda of the Guggenheim houses temporary exhibitions. The permanent collection and contemporary works of art are exhibited in galleries off the tower.*

*A colourful work of art typical of Roy Lichtenstein.*

*'I want a temple to the spirit.' This is how the sponsor Solomon R. Guggenheim presented his project to the architect Frank Lloyd Wright. The resulting museum was built between 1943 and 1959.*

In all, some 5000 sculptures and paintings, including 75 Impressionist masterpieces, are on display. Keen interest in the Guggenheim Museum has led to a number of recent additions. Since 1992, the largest collection of Kandinsky canvases in the world has been exhibited in one of the museums annexes in SoHo. Elsewhere, two new Guggenheim museums have opened, one in Venice, the other in Bilbao thanks to the initiative of Peggy, the niece of Solomon. These new museums of modern art, however, have not copied the architectural style of the original.

*The museums along 5th Avenue have some thought-provoking exhibitions.*

Apart from the Guggenheim Museum, lovers of design have a choice of two other establishments separated by a church. The collection at the **National Academy of Design** was begun back in 1825 and now contains almost 6000 works of art by the likes of Soyer, Eakins and Frank Lloyd Wright. The **Cooper-Hewitt Museum**, meanwhile, contains one of the best collections of design, brought together by the Hewitt sisters.

*On a level with 70th Street, the more classical but equally splendid Frick Collection is exhibited in the former residence of the Pittsburg steel magnate Henry Clay Frick.*

*The impressive Cooper-Hewitt Museum is found in an imposing building once owned by A. Carnegie.*

*The Whitney Museum is situated at the corner of Madison Avenue and 74th Street. This modern building was built in 1966 by Marcel Brueur, an exponent of Bauhaus.*

*The collection at the Whitney Museum has many examples of new movements in American art.*

*A still life at the Whitney Museum.*

The **Whitney Museum** is another must for lovers of modern art. Established in 1930 by the sculptress and patron of the arts Gertrude Vanderbilt Whitney, this out-of-the-ordinary museum exhibits collections that have been refused by the Met. This is the place to see works by artists such as George Bellows, Edward Hopper and Alexander Calder.

*In modern art, and particularly pop art, urban imagery is an important source of inspiration. Andy Warhol often used silk screen and photomechanical printing processes, as in* Green Coca-Cola Bottles, *which explores the themes of mass production, affluence and monopoly.*

*At the Met, a detail from the* Portrait of a German Officer *by Marsden Hartley. The face of the officer is reduced to a simple Maltese cross.*

*The calm greenery of Central Park lies in the very heart of New York. In the distance, the towers of the San Remo Apartments.*

C entral Park is a veritable oasis of greenery that provides New-Yorkers with acres of open spaces, lawns, lakes and wooded hills.

*Rollerblading in Central Park.*

# Central Park

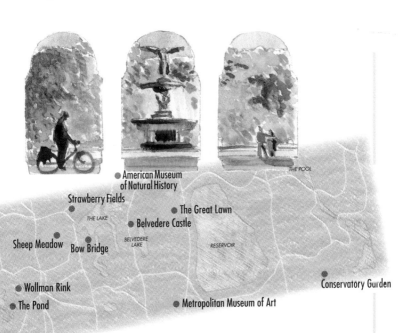

THE POOL

● American Museum of Natural History

Strawberry Fields

THE LAKE

● The Great Lawn

● Belvedere Castle

BELVEDERE LAKE

RESERVOIR

Sheep Meadow ● Bow Bridge

● Wollman Rink

● The Pond

Conservatory Garden ●

● Metropolitan Museum of Art

*A spot of fishing on one of the lakes in Central Park.*

*One of the best views over the park is from the terraces of the medieval Belvedere Castle.*

*A small tear-shaped plot of land, Strawberry Fields, calls to mind the magical universe of John Lennon who lived not far away.*

This haven of peace, closed to cars at the weekend, is the retreat of walkers, cyclists, horse riders and rollerbladers. For a less energetic way of discovering the park, visitors can take one of the traditional horse-drawn carriages from Grand Army Plaza. At the centre of this European-style square stands the Pulitzer Fountain, whilst in the heart of the park another water feature bearing the 'Angel of the Waters' recalls the biblical angel of the Bethesda Fountain in Jerusalem.

*At the heart of Central Park, the Bethesda Fountain (1873) overlooks a terrace frequented by street artists at the edge of the Ramble, a wooded haven for birds.*

*On the grass of the Great Lawn, picnickers sometimes have to make room for music lovers: the Rolling Stones performed a famous concert here in 1969.*

*A detail from the Pulitzer Fountain.*

In summer, in the middle of Central park, the beautiful lawns of **Sheep Meadow** are taken over by chess and croquet enthusiasts who play their favourite games surrounded by various sun-worshippers, picnicking families and frisbee throwers. As for baseball players, they prefer to meet on the **Great Lawn**, which has also been known to host rock concerts and the occasional opera.

*Baseball is one of the most popular sports in America, and a veritable institution. During the baseball season (from April to September) families descend on the Yankee Stadium, home of the New York Yankees, and Shea Stadium, the preserve of the Mets.*

**97**

*Mounted police patrol New York throughout the day and night.*

*Each year, model boat races are organized on Conservatory Water.*

*Central Park West is lined with luxury apartment blocks, such as the San Remo and the Century.*

New Yorkers are particularly fond of the open spaces and greenery of Central Park where they come in their thousands to get away from the hustle and bustle of city life. Natural though it may seem, the park is in fact the result of a huge building project that took place in the 19th century. Over a period of ten years, millions of tonnes of soil and 500,000 trees and bushes were brought in to transform an area of swampland

*In summer, storytellers gather around the statue of Hans Christian Andersen.*

into this English-style park which covers an area of 840 acres (340 hectares). In winter, the snow-covered paths are taken over by cross-country skiers and the **Reservoir**, the large lake in the centre of the park that is usually full of people boating, is transformed into a huge ice rink. In all seasons, the 4-mile (2.5-kilometre) loop around the edges of the Reservoir is used by hundreds of joggers. This runners' paradise was used as the setting for the film *Marathon Man* in which Dustin Hoffman trains for the **New York Marathon**, held each year on the last Sunday of October.

*There is something of a fairy tale atmosphere to Central Park. Not far from Conservatory Water, the visitor passes 'through the looking-glass' to find bronze statues of Lewis Carroll, Alice, the Mad Hatter and the White Rabbit.*

*Bow Bridge is one of seven bronze bridges in Central Park.*

*The tall Dakota Building was once home to Judy Garland, Lauren Bacall and Boris Karloff (his ghost is said to still haunt the premises). It was in front of this very building, the backdrop to the Roman Polanski film* Rosemary's Baby, *that John Lennon was shot and killed.*

The number of joggers, however, has not frightened off the park's grey squirrels. From the top of the small hills which surround the Pond there are stunning views over the buildings of Central Park West, such as the **San Remo** and its twin towers which contain luxury private apartments. Built shortly before the Depression of the 1930s, this apartment building is one of the most sought-after addresses in the city.

*Dustin Hoffman, Diane Keaton and Paul Simon have all lived at the San Remo. Madonna's application, however, was turned down.*

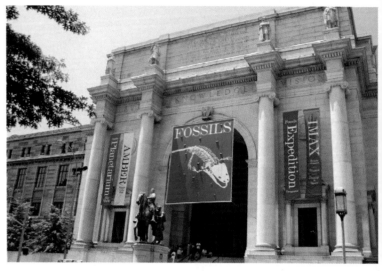

*Opposite Central Park stands the American Museum of Natural History.*

Central Park is every schoolboy's dream of the ideal place in which to play truant, but it is actually used as a playground by children from local private schools who come to visit the zoo or the **American Museum of Natural History**. This museum is the largest of its kind in the world, with 36 million exhibits. Particularly

*A poster of the New York City Ballet.*

*The Lincoln Center for the Performing Arts is a veritable temple to music, dance and theatre. It is built on the 15-acre (6-hectare) site used to film* West Side Story.

*The wall paintings by Marc Chagall at the Metropolitan Opera can only be viewed at night from the outside. During the day, large curtains are drawn to protect them from the sunlight.*

popular among the maze of rooms which cover three blocks are those dedicated to dinosaurs, meteorites and precious stones, as well as the planetarium. Further along, on Upper West Side, the **Lincoln Center** contains seven large per-formance spaces attached to which is the famous Julliard School of Music as featured in the film *Fame*.

*Five large arches form the façade of the Metropolitan Opera, opening into a Modern Art-style palace. The impressive crystal chandeliers, marble staircase and miles of red carpet have played host to some of the most famous divas of this century including Maria Callas.*

*Graffiti expressing the hopes and despair of the Afro-American community. Gang warfare may be a reality in Harlem but there is more to the area than just violence.*

**D**ue to its poor reputation, the area of Harlem is often avoided by tourists but, along with the Cloisters, it is well worth a visit.

*A future Michael Jordan?*

# Harlem

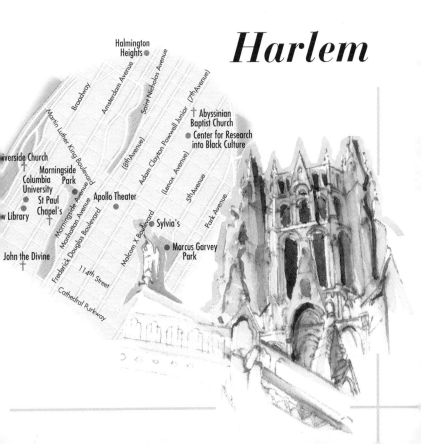

*The grocery shops of Harlem recall those of the Deep South.*

*On Morningside Drive stands the church of Notre Dame, built by the local French community. The altar contains a copy of the grotto at Lourdes that was donated by a woman whose son was miraculously cured.*

True, Harlem has a bad reputation, and many White New Yorkers will be quick to point out its dangers. Nowadays, however, the ghetto is little more than a thing of the past and the Black capital of America, with its African markets, has more to offer than the terrible reputation that reflects just one aspect of it. The rundown streets and 'brownstones' in dark brick with their front steps retain something of the era when Harlem was a

*In the heart of the concrete jungle, the artistic quality of the graffiti speaks for itself.*

prestigious district. As the name indicates, Harlem was originally a Dutch village. During the 19th century, intellectuals and Black musicians moved into the neighbourhood and venues like the **Cotton Club** and the **Apollo** made a name for themselves with performances by the likes of Charlie Parker, Duke Ellington and Cab Calloway. Following the Depression of the 1930s, however, the middle classes moved away from the area to the outskirts of the city. Refurbished in the 1980s, the Apollo was saved from closure and remains the Mecca of Black American music.

*When it opened in 1914, the Apollo Theater was reserved for Whites, but became legendary in 1934 when Blacks were admitted for the first time. A clapometer was used to chose the winners of 'amateur night'.*

*The streets of Harlem are lined with 'brownstones' and businesses.*

*On Sundays, the famous gospel music is sung at the Abyssinian Baptist Church, the oldest Black parish in New York (1808).*

*Before leaving Harlem, a large number of White property owners set fire to their homes in order to claim on the insurance.*

During the 1960s, Harlem became the centre of the fight for Black equality. The Riverside Church on 122nd Street was the scene of sermons by Martin Luther King, whilst on 166th Street, the Audubon Ballroom is the theatre in which Malcolm X, the rebel leader of the Black Muslims, was assassinated. These events led to the decline of Harlem, causing large numbers of White property owners to move out.

*The legend of jazz lives on thanks to artists such as Billie Holiday, pictured here, Charlie 'Bird' Parker and Dizzy Gillespie.*

*Several generations of jazzmen have passed through Harlem, bringing with them different styles from swing and free jazz to bebop.*

*Jazz and Creole food feature on the menu at Sylvia's.*

Today, however, Harlem is rising once more from the ashes. In Hamilton Heights, the new Black middle class has kick-started the local economy. Supermarkets and banks are now all reopening and the **Schomburg Center for Research into Black Culture**, an Afro-American cultural centre, welcomes thousands of visitors each year. This renewed success is personified by the rise of the Black stars of American basketball.

*The one thing that unifies this community, often stricken by unemployment and drugs, is religion. More than just a place of worship, the church also offers a number of different training courses. Negro spirituals and the sermons of the pasteur regularly whip the faithful into a religious frenzy.*

*At the centre of Columbia University's campus stands the Low Memorial Library.*

*In the grounds of the university, St Paul's Chapel is famous for its superb acoustics and it regularly holds lunchtime organ recitals free of charge. Built in 1904, the red brick vaulting of this chapel is bathed in divine light. Along with the neoclassical*

*Low Library and the Hamilton Rotunda, it is generally considered to be one of the university's most beautiful buildings.*

Far from the violence of life on the streets, the campus of **Columbia University**, one of the most prestigious in the country, spreads out over Morningside Heights. Past scholars include over 50 Nobel Prize winners. Here, in the ancient Low Library, students are able to dream of the famous writers who went before them and of becoming

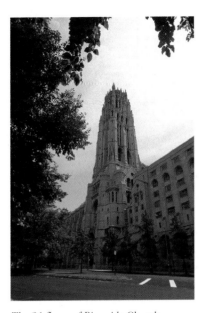

*The 21 floors of Riverside Church.*

*On Riverside, the tomb of the 18th President of the United States, Ulysses S. Grant, was financed by a hundred thousand Americans. Their money made it possible to build this copy of the mausoleum at Halicarnassus.*

*The columns of St John the Divine are a celebration of both Christianity and New York city planning.*

the next Isaac Asimov or J. D. Salinger, the author of *Catcher in the Rye*. Not far from the university, St John the Divine Cathedral once strove to become the largest Christian building in the world. Even though it is only two-thirds complete, this structure that combines Roman and neo-Gothic architecture can still hold a congregation of 10,000.

*In order to complete building work on the imposing cathedral of St John the Divine, architects continue to use building techniques dating back to the Middle Ages. Partly financed by the Rockefeller family, work on a Roman-style building began in 1892. In 1911, a neo-Gothic façade was added. The inside of the Cathedral is over 590 feet (180 metres) long and 145 feet (45 metres) wide.*

*The Cuxa Cloister was brought to New York from the south of France.*

*This ambitious project was financed by John D. Rockefeller who wished to bring a little bit of European history to America.*

*The collection, brought together by the sculptor George Barnard, includes such treasures as the Licorne tapestries, woven in Brussels in 1450.*

To the north of the district, on the banks of the Harlem River, a visit to the **Cloisters** takes on a somewhat anachronistic feel. What a surprise to find cloisters dating from the Middle Ages in the heart of New York! This annexe of the Metropolitan Museum of Art was opened in 1938 and built in medieval style in order to present its collections of architectural pieces, tapestries and stained-glass windows in the most appropriate setting.

*These European cloisters dating back to the Middle Ages were taken to pieces and rebuilt stone by stone on American soil between 1934 and 1938.*

*Size and decadence: elegant Victorian-style houses contrast sharply with this curvaceous figure on a huge mural.*

The hustle and bustle of New York's streets will make your head spin as wealth and poverty shamelessly mix before your eyes.

*The famous yellow cabs.*

# *Street Life*

Whichever part of the world you come from, and whatever your interests, New York promises to captivate. The 'city of lights', as Frank Sinatra called it, is certain to live up to your expectations. Its famous tall skyscrapers, musicals and jazz have all been exported throughout the world but truly come into their own in the city that saw their creation. This, at least, was the opinion of the French philosopher Jean-Paul Sartre who declared on his arrival in the city: 'Jazz is like bananas, all the better for being sampled where it is produced!'

*On the walls of New York, murals are blithely painted one on top of the other.*

*The eccentricity and exuberance of New Yorkers is apparent everywhere you look. It would appear that anything goes, from odd-looking outfits and aggressive haircuts to sports (pictured right) that you don't normally see in the middle of the street!*

Even to the first-time visitor, the streets of New York seem all too familiar. The yellow cabs with their cosmopolitan drivers, the noises of the subway, the smoke coming up through manhole covers in the ground, the massive billboards, the scream of ambulance sirens and the frantic activity all recall the images that are so often to be seen in the American films and television series that are exported throughout the world.

*It's far from being a dog's life living in New York, in spite of the rather harsh climate and frantic pace.*

*Never judge a book by its cover. Is this a police officer who has gone off the rails?*
*A street artist making fun of the uniform? Or a homeless person? Difficult to tell.*

*Gleaming trucks, complete with chromework and horns, rule the streets.*

The capital of all that is large and diverse covers an area of 500 miles² (800 kilometres²), consisting of an almost perfect grid of numbered streets and avenues. Ten million people live in this ordered yet chaotic world in which sharp contrasts await to surprise the visitor. As you make your way through the streets, a delicate church, sculpted like fine lace, crouches in the shadow of an enormous glass and metal structure.

*The New York subway covers more than 706 miles (1142 kms). Tokens are used as tickets and its 469 stations are indicated by either green balls if they sell tokens day and night or red balls if they do not. A word of caution: express trains do not stop at every station.*

*The East River is dotted with loud and colourful signal stations.*

Each year, over a hundred thousand new immigrants arrive to try their luck in the promised land. Yuppies in suits pass eccentric-looking artists without even batting an eyelid. Who can tell if behind the craggy faces of the homeless hides a former successful businessman or fallen music-hall star? In spite of such poverty, New York is a city that likes to party. The grid of streets provides a grandiose setting for the many **parades** that are

*The River Café stands on the banks of the East River.*

Art galleries such as Leo Castelli's and the Mary Boone Gallery have made SoHo what it is today. A free guide to all art exhibitions is published in the monthly Art Now Gallery Guide.

organized for various events. Complete with costumes, floats, fanfares and confetti, New Yorkers celebrate all festivals enthusiastically accompanied by a mass of fireworks and Star-Spangled Banners. Such rituals have been part of the American way of life since the celebration of La Fayette in 1824. The most impressive parades are these that take place each year at Easter (on Easter Sunday) and to celebrate Halloween (31 October), Martin Luther King Day (third Sunday in May), St Patrick's Day (17 March), Gay Pride (late June) and Thanksgiving (fourth Thursday in November).

*The façade of the Eagle Warehouse, in Columbia Heights, in the heart of Brooklyn.*

*Only yellow taxis are licensed. The tariffs are shown on the front right-hand door and the meters issue printed receipts. There is an initial charge of $2, then 30 cents per 1/5 mile (320 metres). A 15% tip should be added.*

In Manhattan, each district has its own distinct identity: luxury shops in the Upper East Side, shows and music halls on Broadway, fashionable designers and art galleries in SoHo and Greenwich Village and retail shops in Chelsea. Shops that are slightly off the beaten track can turn out to be veritable Aladdin's caves. They often only last a few months, so the speciality of a district can change overnight. For many years, the former warehouses that line the Hudson River in Chelsea remained empty, but recently a new generation of artists has transformed them into art galleries.

*Eat your heart out Mickey Mouse! A white rat brightens up this old wall.*

Whilst they are not yet truly established, nothing is to say that they will one day not take over from SoHo and TriBeCa. Furthermore, New York is not just Manhattan, even though few tourists venture out into the other boroughs due to their reputation for being dangerous. In the heart of the **Bronx**, for example, in a somewhat post-apocalyptic setting, lies a charming spot that is absolutely safe: the largest city zoo in America.

*There is more to New York than just a city of skyscrapers and glass and metal structures – as grey squirrels of Central Park will testify. From the city zoo of the Bronx and the beaches of Coney Island to the restored district of Richmond, the Big Apple has the ability to surprise and delight.*

*The multiracial population of Brooklyn, the largest of New York's boroughs, includes West Indians, Jews, Koreans and Russians.*

*A former fire station stands at the end of the Brooklyn Bridge.*

In **Brooklyn**, which claims to be 'the fourth-largest city in America', tranquil streets rub shoulders with inner-city poverty. In this cosmopolitan district, each community jealously defends its own territory. In Williamsburg, for example, Orthodox Jews live according to the Hebrew calendar, whilst the elegant Victorian houses on Park Slope are owned by 'Wasps', an acronym that stands for White Anglo-Saxon Protestants.

*Low rents have helped to attract an alternative 'underground' set to Brooklyn. These 20th-century artists often find the inspiration for their work in poverty and inner-city violence.*

*The New York Fire Department is kept busy. The dilapidated state of the city's utilities means that gas leaks and floods are a common occurrence.*

*New York has only the 30th-worst crime rate for a city in the United States. The police patrol day and night on foot, by car and on horseback.*

*Traffic speeds by over three levels.*

*Chess players, particularly those from the Cuban community, regularly gather in parks to play matches outdoors. Lovers of nature should head for the Aquarium at Coney Island or the botanical gardens in the 526 acres (210 hectares) known as Prospect Park.*

At the southern end of Brooklyn lies a seaside resort that is reachable by subway. As soon as the weather turns warm, New Yorkers head for the miles of golden sand on the Atlantic coast at **Coney Island**. The three amusement parks, with their big dipper and big wheel rusted by the spray from the sea, make this one of the largest playgrounds in the world.

*Underprivileged families have set up home along the banks of the Hudson River.*

The borough of **Queens** is the home of Kennedy Airport and venue for the Flushing Meadows tennis tournament. Meanwhile, on Staten Island, there is the wonderfully restored historical district of Richmond which is well worth a visit. From the ferry which takes you there, the view of Manhattan and its skyscrapers is breathtaking.

*In New York, there are almost as many Jews as there are in Israel and more Irish than there are in Dublin. The Afro-American community, the largest minority in the city, totals almost half the population of Senegal. Today it is closely followed by the Asian and Hispanic communities. This 'melting pot' of nationalities and cultures is one of the distinctive features of New York.*

# *Creative Workshop*

*Having discovered the wonders of New York, it's now time to get creative.*

*All you need are a few odds and ends and a little ingenuity to keep the spirit of your adventure alive by creating your own beautiful craft objects.*

*These simple yet ingenious ideas capture the special flavour of New York and leave you with a permanent reminder of your visit.*

*An original, simple and fun way to preserve your holiday memories.*

# Empire State Building Postcard

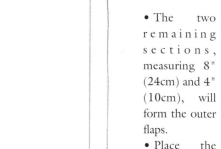

*T*he tall outline of the Empire State Building lends itself perfectly to paper sculpture. This postcard is a fun way of sending greetings to young and old alike.

## Preparation

• To make the postcard you will need a strip of card 24" x 4" (62cm x 10.5cm).

• Enlarge the diagram (right) to the actual size of the postcard using a photocopier.

• The first two sections, which measure 4" (10cm) and 8" (24cm) respectively, will form the two inner flaps of the card.

• The two remaining sections, measuring 8" (24cm) and 4" (10cm), will form the outer flaps.

• Place the photocopy on the sheet of card, tape it in place and cut along the solid lines with a Stanley knife.

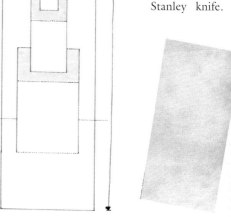

21cm

21cm

62 cm

10cm

10,5cm

## Folding

• Score along the dotted lines using the blunt side of the blade. Fold the card along the scored lines in the direction shown (right)

• Once you have assembled the body of the Empire State Building, paint the sides gold and the roofs black. Allow to dry.

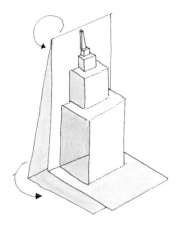

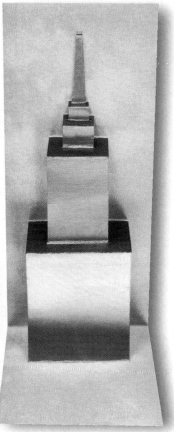

• Finally, stick the inner surfaces of the inner and outer flaps together then close the card and place it under a heavy object to make the folds nice and sharp.

## Materials

• a sheet of 250g card, at least 24" (62cm) long • black and gold paint suitable for use on card • Stanley knife • sticky tape • paper glue

# *Jazz Plate*

*The design needs to be a little smaller than the centre of the plate. Enlarge or reduce the design on a photocopier depending on the size of your plate.*

## Painting the plate

• Position the stencil on the plate and stick it in place using the spray adhesive. This will stop paint leaking under the stencil.

## Making the stencil

• To make the stencil, stick the design onto a sheet of card and cut out the black sections using a Stanley knife.
• Next, cut the stencil to fit the centre of the plate.

- Apply the paint by dabbing with a stencil brush. Do not water down the paint: the stronger the colour, the clearer the design will be.
- For additional decoration, musical notes can be painted around the outer edge of the plate.
- Allow to dry.

*This painted plate should not be washed in a dishwasher.*

## Materials

- a white or coloured plate (or set of plates)
- ceramic paints in several colours
- a sheet of 250g card • stencil brush
- Stanley knife • sticky tape • spray adhesive
(of the type used for mounting photographs)

# Number Plate Photo Frame

*T**he design for this photo frame is inspired
by the number plates on New York taxis.*

### Making the stencil

• Enlarge this stylized image of the Statue of Liberty on a photocopier until it is 5" (12.5cm) tall. Place the photocopy on a sheet of card, tape it in place and cut out the black sections using a Stanley knife.

### Making the number plate

• Using the Stanley knife, cut out a rectangle of stiff card measuring approximately 8" x 16" (20cm x 40cm) and round off the corners.

• Paint the cut edges of the rectangle with gesso using a fine brush. Allow to dry completely then spray the entire rectangle silver, paying particular attention to the edges.

• Allow to dry before applying the design of the Statue of Liberty as shown using the stencil and black spray paint.

## Mounting the photos

• Choose three photos of New York, mount them on a sheet of card and cut around each one. Stick a small piece of cardboard onto the back of each photo and glue the other side of the cardboard to the number plate.

## Finishing the frame

• Coat four screws with glue to keep them in position and place them on the number plate as shown, screwing them into the card.

• Tie a piece of string between the two top screws so that the frame can be hung on the wall.

## Materials

• a sheet of stiff cardboard • a sheet of 224g card
• Stanley knife • fine brush • sticky tape • pot of gesso (or matt white acrylic paint) • spray paints in silver and black
• strong all-purpose glue • 4 screws approximately 1/4" (4mm) in diameter and 1" (3cm) long

# The Big Apple

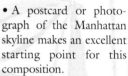

*C*omic strips and modern architecture are two of the favourite themes of contemporary New York artist Roy Lichtenstein. Here is an original picture inspired by the style of this master of pop art which takes as its subject the city's nickname: the Big Apple.

- A postcard or photograph of the Manhattan skyline makes an excellent starting point for this composition.
- Using faint lines, draw the outline of the cityscape with the apple in the background.
- Roy Lichtenstein's work is instantly recognizable by his use of solid blocks of pure bright colour, black outlines around shapes and stippling to represent light areas.
- Paint the apple bright red to set the tone for the rest of the picture. Apply the colour as a solid block without trying to represent light and shade.
- When it comes to the buildings, however, the light sides are suggested by stippling whilst the sides in the shade are painted in solid blocks of a single colour.
- Paint the bushes in a fairly strong green, using a softer green for the apple leaf. For the foreground,

which is actually an expanse of water, use yellow rather than blue in order to set off the buildings to greater effect.

• Use a touch of ochre for the stalk of the apple and add the only shading in the whole picture: a long stroke of darker green on the apple leaf.

• Acrylic colours dry quickly, so wait until each colour is dry before applying the next.

• Finish off the picture by outlining all the painted areas in black. The thickness of the lines should vary and be left out where the 3-D effect is more convincing without an outline, as on the buildings.

• Add a few touches of black to the apple to suggest its curved shape and paint a black line all around the edge of your picture.

## Materials

• a sheet of 280g watercolour paper • acrylic paints in yellow, ochre, red, two shades of green, blue and black • paintbrush • pencil

# Eggs Benedict

## Preparation

Eggs Benedict are prepared in individual portions, so you will need a small ovenproof dish for each person. Place half a spoonful of hot water in each and heat in the microwave until the water is boiling.